To Dr. Bjornbak,

Thank you for all your care and concern.

I hope this book gives you a bit of peace and hope.

With kindest wishes and greatest blessings,

Rosie Clardon

April 20, 2018

TURN ON
HOPE STREET

Stories, Faith and

Neuroscience

ROSIE CLANDOS

In honor of my dad, Bruno (Barney) Zoladz

In honor of my mom, Mary Natalie Vujnovich Zoladz

Dedicated

To my family and friends

To people who struggle to live fuller, happier lives

Contents

Forward

This is how it started. In 2008, I was writing an article for the *Los Angeles Times* about learning and stress. One of the neuroscientists I interviewed was Eric Kandel, a Nobel Laureate who researched memory storage in brain cells.

He explained that repeated thoughts, words, and behaviors related to hope, love, and happiness can change the structure and function of the brain. In the same way, repeated thoughts, words, and behaviors related to fear, stress, and anxiety can change the brain.

Did I hear right?! Neuroplasticity was coming into public awareness at that time, and I wanted to confirm my understanding. I rephrased my question. Same answer, different words. By the fourth time, Kandel was laughing. When I got off the phone, I was dancing.

I imagined that neuroplasticity was like walking on a path in the woods. If I frequently walked on that path, it would become wider, and the ground would be firmer.

Neuroplasticity explained a lot in my life. For one thing, it meant that prayer could actually, *physically* change the brain. I was thrilled.

The realization gave me hope.

For years, I had been saying all kinds of prayers, for all kinds of reasons, and in all kinds of ways. Some prayers were answered – others were not. But this news made me understand that my brain is actually changing when I pray.

I conducted another important interview with psychiatrist and PTSD trauma expert Kerry Ressler. At Harvard, he had been a student of the Nobel Laureate Linda Buck. I asked Ressler about the amount of electrical energy used by the brain when a person tries to stop experiencing angry or fearful thoughts, and instead, feel peaceful ones.

"A LOT!!" he said. But there was no way to measure that energy at the time.

His answer was important because I had thought that praying involved asking God to give me something, or to change a situation, or to help me change a situation.

But maybe I had to do more – like "renew my mind", as some people say. And that may take repeated thoughts, speech, and behaviors. That means work.

Long-term changes to the brain, to our beliefs, and to our behaviors often happen slowly. But changes can occur very quickly when a trauma, shock, or highly emotional event is involved. They also occur with disease or injury.

In addition to changing ourselves, renewing our minds may affect people around us. One of Newton's laws states: For every action, there is an equal or opposite reaction.

For example, when we show empathy or compassion, then mirror neurons are understood to trigger similar "contagious" emotions in most people. Other strong emotions such as fear and hate can be contagious, too.

Part of praying involves belief. For some people, that's easy – possibly because of their biology or life experiences. But other people may need to try very hard to believe and imagine a positive outcome.

I like to compare the effort of repeatedly *believing* in God for answers to the effort of repeatedly *begging* God for answers. Repeatedly *begging* for an answer to a prayer can eventually make me feel hopeless. Belief has to be part of my picture.

It may take energy to believe *or* beg for something you don't see or that doesn't seem possible. But in the long run, hope and optimism take less work – and may be healthier.

Believing in a positive outcome improves the neural circuits in our brains, those that may otherwise worsen as we age, according to research by psychiatrist Jose Pardo in *Neuroimage*, in April 2007.

Plus, optimism plays a role in self-care and management of chronic illness, according to a research study led by Marion Fournier and published in the *Behavioral Journal of Health Psychology* in November 2002.

Further, having a positive emotional style has been shown to predict resistance to colds and viruses, reports Sheldon Cohen and his research team in an article published by *Psychosomatic Medicine* in July 2003.

This book is based on my belief that God has given each of us a brain, the ability to change, and the option to choose and believe – *anything* – good or bad.

And with that comes a sobering point. Neuroscientist Kandel grew up in Austria, and he was nine years old when Nazis took over the country in 1938. After his non-Jewish friends and classmates heard repeated messages of hate, they would become his tormentors.

For good or evil – that's neuroplasticity.

Introduction

True story. Told with permission. Name changed.

Sarah heard a powerful sermon about worrying. The well-meaning preacher said, "Stop thinking! Stop depending on your own reasoning! When you're depending on your own reasoning, you're denying God's power!"

Sarah was overwhelmed by the clutter in her house.

So she did exactly what the preacher said.

She prayed. (Good.)

She trusted in God's power. (Good.)

She believed in a positive outcome. (Good.)

She could even imagine her house looking clean and comfy. (Good.)

She felt peaceful after praying. (Nice.)

She was confident she'd overcome the habit she hated. (Nice.)

When she'd feel overwhelmed, she would pray again. (Good.)

I have known my friend Sarah for ten years. She has not yet changed. Since she moved to a smaller place, she spends most of her time while at home in a small area around her bed. The clutter is overwhelming.

What's the problem?

Maybe she stopped reasoning. Maybe she stopped questioning.

"Why hasn't my prayer been answered?"

"What am I doing wrong here?"

"When is this going to change?"

Sarah had heard so many messages about not thinking when overwhelmed that the messages had taken root. She really did stop reasoning when she was overwhelmed. She stopped problem-solving.

Now this is important. Sarah is a smart woman with four academic degrees including a doctorate in psychology. At other times, she is an astute, critical thinker with excellent communication skills. Yet, she couldn't understand how the idea of neuroplasticity could help her. That was for *other* people.

Granted, this woman hates housekeeping and she doesn't hesitate to admit that she procrastinates. So the message about not thinking, not doing something, and only trusting God fit comfortably into her existing viewpoint about housecleaning. Someone else might have prayed, trusted God, *and* cleaned the house.

But her error is a common one. There's a human tendency to take information that fits into our current way of life or philosophy and discard the rest.

Let's back up for a moment and give the preacher some credit. According to Sarah, the other half of the preacher's message was a very helpful one about getting close to God. Sarah said she loves doing this. She also loves to laugh. Although she gave some funny and plausible reasons for her habits, she said she still had a hard time changing them.

I'll explain something here about a few parts of the brain.

- Worrying entails allowing our minds to dwell on problems. It involves fear, anxiety, or anger. Those strong emotions trigger activity in the brain area called the amygdala.
- Trusting in God involves ignoring worries, and instead *thinking* about God. This, or meditation, *reduces* activity in the anterior cingulate cortex. (However, high activity in this brain area is related to obsessive compulsive disorder.)
- Critical thinking and problem solving involve asking questions, associating ideas, evaluating, and decision-making. That's done in the frontal lobes of the brain.
- Remembering facts, scripture verses, school lessons, or similar information is largely done in the hippocampus.

- Synchronized thinking, Ahhh! That's like an orchestra performing beautiful music. The violins trigger deep emotions. The flutes give hope. The percussion section flames courage. The brass section makes us feel decisive. The one-note ting of a bell makes us smile. The intricate and complicated movements of the pianist cause us to think, "Where is she going with this?"

The orchestra is like the whole brain – the whole brain that God created. The brain that has many parts, and they can work together for good. This wonderful brain can help people praise God, create life-saving drugs, design aircraft, remember stories to tell their grandchildren, and feel love and compassion.

When a person takes a little time to meditate or pray to a loving God, certain brain chemicals are released. These chemicals increase our ability to relax, learn, and reason. They reduce the negative effects of cortisol, the "stress" chemical, which can slow down learning.

After meditation or prayer, a person can go back to problem-solving activities, and their decision-making may be easier and better.

When parts of the brain stop working together, problems may occur. They might be psychological, emotional, physical, or educational. But when *we stop* using our brains to think critically, we open the door for trouble.

I bet that's not what the preacher intended for Sarah or the audience. Reasoning and thinking are part of God's provision for us. They're gifts.

To create new habits, we can use Bible verses related to the qualities and behaviors we want – patience, self-control, kindness, love, joy, generosity, persistence, courage, forgiveness, or hope.

When we frequently repeat those scriptures, think about them, and _act_ on them, we can change our brains!

Ahhh! That's using neuroplasticity – for good.

When Sarah understood this, the lights went on. She had hope.

And that's what I'm offering in this book.

About This Book

Each chapter contains three short sections: stories, scriptures, and science. There's space in each chapter for your notes or personal affirmations. The science section simply provides more information about the brain or topic. These three separate sections engage different areas of the brain, and they can increase learning.

At the end of this book, you'll find some helpful resources and several tip sheets that relate to the stories.

Happy reading!

Chapter 1

Kindness vs. Harshness

My dad was a generous guy who was helpful, curious, creative, and thoughtful. He loved learning, even though he never graduated from high school.

During our visits, we'd go to libraries. Or we'd walk arm-in-arm in pretty neighborhoods in Michigan or California, pretending that we lived near each other in cute little houses with flower gardens.

But if he was upset or sick, I would act and speak very cautiously.

When he was receiving treatment for liver cancer, the nurses said that he was the model patient. But when treatment failed and he became seriously ill, he had a difficult time. His pain increased, he could barely eat, and he couldn't sleep.

I came back to Detroit to help him for awhile. When I walked into his house, he was in a bad mood. "What are you doing here?!"

His neighborhood was unsafe, and I couldn't park my sister's new car there overnight. He said I should stay at her house.

I knew my dad cared about me. But after a while, it was difficult to cope with his strong emotions and my old memories.

Back home in California, I attended a church where the pastor talked about blessing people, especially those who upset us. That sounded good, but I seldom did it.

While in Detroit that Sunday, I went to an African-American church. I had visited many churches in Los Angeles. In churches where the needs were greater, I often saw that faith was stronger.

That Sunday in Detroit, I was inspired by the music, lyrics, and people who danced as they thanked God. Afterward, some women prayed with me. They encouraged me to bless my dad.

Later that day as he was yelling in the living room, I took advantage of his poor hearing. I knew he couldn't hear me while I was cooking his meal. So I passionately repeated sentences aloud, like this: "Lord, please bless him with peace, bless him with kindness.... I bless him…. I bless you, Dad, with love. You are kind and loving, Dad…."

By the time I brought the food to him, I felt pretty good. What happened next shocked me.

He apologized!

"I'm so sorry, so so sorry, Rosie…. I just feel so sick…."

The love and compassion that I felt for him amazed me. Soon after, when I looked out the window, his neighborhood didn't seem so ugly. And I felt compassion for the other people who lived there.

Later, I would cherish his apology and deeply understand how pain could translate into anger.

* * *

For a short time when I was in high school, I worked the midnight shift at Biff's Restaurant near the Fisher Building in Detroit.

In the middle of one night, I wondered how I'd make it through the upcoming day. Around 6:00 a.m., a man came in and sat in a closed area of the restaurant. I explained that he'd have to sit somewhere else. He politely asked again. And again, I said no and gave him a dirty look.

The owner gently intervened, "It's OK. Let him sit there."

I was embarrassed. The customer talked kindly to me as I brought him coffee, but I was aloof. When he got up to leave, I saw that he had given me a tip. It was five times larger than his bill.

The man's kindness in the midst of my rudeness made me feel so sad. He must have seen the pain below the surface of my behavior. I had to fight back my tears.

I wish I could have told him how much his kindness meant to me. Maybe he saw my eyes.

Chapter 1: Kindness vs. Harshness

Scriptures and Affirmations

Honor goes to kind and gracious men, mere money goes to cruel men. Proverbs 11:16 (LB)

- I imagine acting kind and gracious to myself and other people. When I treat myself with respect, I honor myself.

Some people like to make cutting remarks, but the words of the wise soothe and heal. Proverbs 12:18 (LB)

- I speak lovingly and kindly to myself and others. My words help to soothe and restore me and them.

Anxious hearts are very heavy, but a word of encouragement does wonders. Proverbs 12:25 (LB)

- When I'm upset, I speak encouraging words to myself. They lighten my heart and my mood. They can do the same for other people.

Pleasant words are a honeycomb, sweet to the soul and healing to the bones. Proverbs 16:24 (LB)

- Speaking kindly to myself and other people makes me feel good and healthy.

Love forgets mistakes. Nagging about them parts the best of friends. Proverbs 17:9 (LB)

- I love myself so I learn from my mistakes. I refuse to hurt myself by berating myself about my errors.

Try to show as much compassion as your Father does. Never criticize or condemn, or it will all come back on you. Luke 6:36 (LB)

- I'm compassionate with myself. God has compassion for me. I don't criticize or condemn myself and other people. Compassion will make me feel better.

You must love others as much as yourself. No other commandments are greater than these. Mark 12:31 (LB)

- I love my neighbor, and I love myself. If I can't love myself, how can I love anyone else?

NOTES

More space is provided at the back of the book for your own thoughts.

Chapter 1: Kindness vs. Harshness

Related Science

Compassionate thoughts and feelings motivate people to act compassionately.

- Ashar, Y., Andrews-Hanna, et al. (2016). Effects of compassion meditation on a psychological model of charitable donation. *Emotion,* 16(5): 691-705.

Many of the brain's structures and functions can be permanently altered by excessive fear or anger – which can reduce our ability to properly remember and reason. In turn, these alterations affect decision-making and responses to people.

- Davidson, R. J., Lewis, D. A., et al. (2002). Neural and behavioral substrates of mood and mood regulation. *Biological Psychiatry*, 52(6): 478-502.

Research shows that one way to reduce anger and frustration is to replace negative thoughts with positive ones.

- Dua, J. and Price, I. (1993). Effectiveness of training in negative thought reduction and positive thought increment in reducing thought-produced distress. *Journal of Genetic Psychology,* 154(1): 97-109.

Chapter 1: Kindness vs. Harshness

Here are some useful definitions and important tips.

1. **Neuron: brain cell**. The brain has more than 100 billion neurons. They work together so we can live and learn.

2. **Dendrite: tiny branch on a neuron**. When we practice new information or a new skill, dendrites on neurons grow close to other neurons. Dendrites *receive* information from other neurons.

3. **Axon: tiny fiber on a neuron.** Axons *send* information to other neurons, muscles, and glands.

4. **Synapse: tiny space between neurons.** Information moves from one neuron to another by crossing these spaces.

5. **Neurotransmitter: brain chemical**. These chemicals mix with small amounts of electricity to send messages across the synapse spaces. These messages tell our brains and bodies what to do.

6. **Neuroplasticity: the brain's ability to change**. When neurons in different areas of the brain are

activated at the same time, a pathway or circuit may be created. When those circuits are strengthened or redirected, the brain changes. Neuroplasticity can occur with repeated speech, thoughts, and actions. Also, it can happen with disease, injury, or changes in the environment.

***This is important*:** When we feel anxiety, depression, or anger, then certain chemicals cause some messages to move very slowly. Specifically, messages about schoolwork and other *non-survival* topics cannot travel quickly in the brain. These messages can't easily cross the synapses and connect to other neurons. Then we have a hard time concentrating! That's a big problem for many people who have a lot of stress in their lives.

When we're upset, we can *do* things to feel positive emotions. Exercise, deep breathing, meditation, praying, or saying positive affirmations can make it easier to learn, remember, or make decisions.

This is even more important: When we feel hope, peace, or other positive emotions, then different chemicals cause messages to move quickly. Messages hurry across the synapses and connect to the appropriate neurons. Then we learn faster. We remember more. We can think creatively.

This explains *one* reason why praying can be so effective, especially before making decisions.

Chapter 2

Forgiveness vs. Anger

When terrorists attacked the World Trade Center, I asked my pastor, "Shouldn't we be praying for the terrorists?" He looked disturbed. Still, I wondered: How *could* we possibly pray? I had read about praying for your enemies, not cursing them.

I would base my own answer on the following events. When I was 21, I moved from Detroit to Los Angeles. On my first Saturday there, I ate dinner in a restaurant and chatted for a long time with the people next to me.

Walking back to my hotel room and passing lovely homes, I was so happy to see that trees still had leaves, and flowers were blooming still at Thanksgiving time.

Suddenly, a man grabbed me and pressed a knife against my chest. He said, "This is a rape."

Later that night, police drove me to a hospital.

The next morning I met with a therapist and expressed violent hatred for the man. For months, I did that, and I imagined fighting him.

Three years later, I walked into the small lobby of my office building, and I heard a commotion. I saw my co-worker with her head bent down on her desk. She was saying, "I can't see you. I don't know what you look like."

Just then, two men stepped out from behind a wall. One man had a small gun. (I thought it wasn't real.) He tried to yank my wallet from my hand. Furious, I struggled with him. He got away with the wallet, but nothing else from me.

The following year I received an envelope without a return address. Inside the envelope was a small picture of my sister Patty wearing her high school graduation cap.

Since infancy, she had an enlarged head due to hydrocephalus, water pressure on the brain. On the other side of the picture was a message that she had written to me in her wiggly handwriting. Her picture along with some ID and five dollars were the only things that had been in my stolen wallet.

I often wondered if the man felt sorry when he saw the picture of Patty. When I'd imagine him feeling some compassion for my sister, I'd have a little feeling of kindness for him.

One day I had a thought about praying for him. I prayed that he wouldn't rob people. That made me think of praying for the rapist. NO! A horrible thought!!!! I couldn't.

But then – maybe I could pray that he wouldn't hurt other women, or he would get help for his problem, or he would have self-control, or he would have compassion for women. I did what I never thought possible – I prayed for him.

* * *

Recently, I asked someone about the secret of her 30-year marriage. "Pick your battles," she said. Then she asked if I was married, and if I had a secret. I'm not, and I do.

It's a post-marriage secret: Bless your husband when you're upset with him. Pray that he would have the opposite behavior. Pray in Jesus' name.

I do not suggest just a short, measly prayer. No, no. Rather, a spoken prayer so you can hear yourself, and a prayer that involves physical movement, such as walking or housework. Then electrical energy in the brain can more easily shift from the amygdala – the area related to the fight, flight, and freeze response – to a few other brain areas that process forgiveness, empathy and reasoning.

To overcome recurrent negative memories, I suggest repeating those prayers. Forgiveness sometimes happens in layers. Of course, deal with the issues, but often repetitive negative thoughts can magnify problems.

Looking back, I've often wondered what would have happened if I'd had more empathy for important people in my life. Would that have activated their mirror neurons, those brain cells that trigger corresponding emotions? In turn, would they have felt more empathy toward me? Who knows?

And who knows what might happen with others – people in the news, for example. Would it help to bless them with truth, self-control, compassion, wisdom, and all that other good stuff?

In those cases, there would be no influence from mirror neurons – only from God.

Chapter 2: Forgiveness vs. Anger

Scriptures and Affirmations

You've heard it said, "Love your neighbor and hate your enemy." But I tell you: Love your enemies and pray for those who persecute you. Matthew 5:43 (NIV)

- I will pray for people who make me upset. I know that when I bless them, I'll feel better.

Don't be bewildered or surprised when you go through the fiery trials ahead, for this is no strange, unusual thing that is going to happen to you. 1 Peter 4:12 (LB)

- I'm not surprised when life is difficult. Problems are normal. They can help me depend on God as I look for solutions.

Do not be overcome by evil, but overcome evil with good. Romans 12:21 (LB)

- By forgiving people, it will help me overcome revenge, hatred, bitterness, and anything else that is negative.

The Lord works righteousness for those who are oppressed. Psalm 103:6 (NIV)

- I choose to believe that God will help me with problems and provide justice when I'm treated unfairly.

Cast your cares on the Lord and he will sustain you; he will never let the righteous fall. Psalm 55:22 (NIV)

- I imagine giving my problems to God each day. He carries them and helps me.

NOTES

Chapter 2: Forgiveness vs. Anger

Related Science

Expressions of compassion or empathy can reduce aggression or conflict in relationships.

- Richardson, D. R., Hammock, G. S., et al. (1994). Empathy as a cognitive inhibitor of interpersonal aggression. *Aggressive Behavior,* (20)4: 275-289.

War survivors and violent-crime victims who forgive those responsible for their pain have decreased depression and anxiety. However, people who don't forgive have an increased likelihood of psychiatric disease.

- Spiers, A. (2004). Forgiveness as a secondary prevention strategy for victims of interpersonal crime. *Australasian Psychiatry,* 12(3): 261-263.

In a research study, people who experienced severe adversities were more likely to feel compassion and empathize with other people in stressful situations. The more compassion they felt, the more they did for other people.

- Lim, D. and DeSteno, D. (2016). Suffering and compassion. The links among adverse life experiences, empathy, compassion, and prosocial behavior. *Emotion,* doi: 10.1037/emo0000144

Some people who have had negative experiences may *lack* compassion for others who have had similar negative experiences. It may be difficult or disturbing to accurately recall the effort required to overcome trauma, pain, or distress.

- Ruttan, R., McDonnell, MH., et al. (2015). When having "been there" doesn't mean I care: When prior experience reduces compassion for emotional distress. *Journal of Personality and Social Psychology,* 108(4): 610-622.

Chapter 3

Gratitude vs. Bitterness

In West Hollywood, I used to eat in a deli where the man working behind the counter joked with customers in his Eastern European accent.

One day I asked him, "How can you be so friendly all the time?"

"Why do you ask?"

His shirt sleeve was rolled up, and I could see the imprint made by Nazis in a concentration camp.

"You have numbers on your arm," I said softly.

He stretched out his arms and said, "I'm alive! I make a choice to be happy!"

* * *

I visited my sister Patty in Detroit while she was living in a nursing home, although she was only 31 years old. When she was an infant, a smallpox vaccination caused encephalitis then hydrocephalus. Slowly, water pressure accumulated on her brain. Ultimately, it would destroy major parts of it.

In the hallways of the nursing home, there were lost-looking patients, bad smells, and cockroaches.

When I entered Patty's room, she was surprised and immediately turned to a picture of Jesus on her wall and whispered, "Thank you."

Under the picture, there was a box of expensive chocolates that someone had given her. Patty LOVED chocolates.

After ten days, I needed to return to Los Angeles. We hugged and cried. Patty kept thanking me for visiting her.

When I finally turned away to leave, Patty called me back.

"Here, please take this." It was her box of chocolates.

"I can't. No, you keep it."

"Please, please, you have to take it."

Back and forth we went. She finally demanded that I take them. In all my life, I have never received such a generous gift.

* * *

Patty often called and begged me to move her to California. It was taking me a long time to find the right nursing home that could meet her needs and would accept her. One day I spoke to Patty and she sounded fine, but the next time we talked, her words were garbled.

The staff said that she was obstinate, and she refused to move her arm. I frantically tried to get a physician to see her. After a week, he finally visited her. She had had a stroke.

A social worker in Los Angeles encouraged me to quickly arrange for Patty and my mom to move. Patty would require lots of medical care to help with the effects of the hydrocephalus and the stroke.

At the nursing home that we'd finally found for Patty, we met psychologist Stan Peterson. Patty and I didn't know what to make of him.

She struggled to say, "Is that guy for real, or what?"

The staff and patients loved him. He often made kind comments about their accomplishments – big or small.

One day, Stan told me that he'd been in a serious motor cycle accident when he was 21. When he came out of the coma, he had total amnesia. He didn't recognize his mother or anyone else. He needed to relearn everything, including the alphabet.

After a lot of hard work, Stan went back to college and then became a psychologist, helping patients who had brain injuries and other problems.

His extreme appreciation finally made sense to us. He was a role-model for encouraging people and appreciating victories of any size.

* * *

When Patty's condition worsened further, she was moved to a different nursing home. Now she was blind and paralyzed, except for her left arm. Unable to swallow well, she was fed through a gastrointestinal tube. She rarely spoke. Seeing Patty in this condition was extremely upsetting. But it was devastating to remember her as a young girl, frightened about the likely progression of her condition.

Her nursing assistant was Rosanna. She spoke lovingly, and she tenderly cared for Patty as if she were a princess. She dispensed blessings like an angel.

"Patty smiled today. It's a blessing!" Rosanna said.

"Patty grabbed my hand when I was changing her. It's a blessing!"

Rosanna's words became ingrained. Long after Patty had passed over to a better life, Rosanna's lessons of appreciation still resonated at surprising times through my life.

"It's a blessing!"

Chapter 3: Gratitude vs. Bitterness

Scriptures and Affirmations

Death and life are in the power of the tongue, and those who choose it will eat its fruit. Proverbs 18:21 (NLV)

- I know that what I say has the power to build or destroy. I have a choice to speak with hate or love, despair or hope, bitterness or gratitude.

Say "thank you" to the Lord for being so good, for always being so loving and kind. Has the Lord redeemed you? Then speak out! Tell others he has saved you from your enemies. Psalm 107:1 (LB)

- I share with other people my gratitude for God's healing, help, and hope.

Give thanks to the Lord, call on his name; make known among the nations what he has done. Psalms 105:1 (NIV)

- I enjoy thanking God for all the wonderful things he does. I tell people about his love and kindness.

Give thanks in all circumstances, for this is God's will for you in Christ Jesus. 1 Thessalonians 5:18 (NIV)

- I look for ways to be thankful, even in difficult times. I believe that God can make something good come out of something bad.

Sing and make music in your heart to the Lord, always give thanks to God for everything, in the name of our Lord Jesus Christ. Ephesians 5:20 (NIV)

- I express gratitude to God by singing, writing, and dancing.

Thanks be to God! He gives us the victory through our Lord Jesus Christ. 1 Corinthians 15:57 (NIV)

- I tell God thank you for helping me overcome challenges through Jesus.

NOTES

Chapter 3: Gratitude vs. Bitterness

Related Science

Gratitude decreases depression and anxiety. In a study involving 224 patients, researchers assessed chronic pain, sleep disturbances, depression, anxiety, and gratitude. The results showed that gratitude helped to reduce depression. Also, there was a positive link between, sleep, gratitude, and reduced anxiety.

- Ng, M. Y. and Wong, W. S. (2013). The differential effects of gratitude and sleep on psychological distress in patients with chronic pain. *Journal of Health Psychology,* 18(2): 263-271.

In two experiments designed to measure the personality trait of gratitude, researchers found that grateful thoughts improved mood and a sense of well-being.

- Watkins, P. C., Woodward, K., et al. (2003). Gratitude and happiness: Development of a measure of gratitude and relationships with subjective well-being. *Social Behavior and Personality,* 31(5): 431-452.

Researchers analyzed two long-term studies and found that when people experience a life transition, gratitude can protect them from depression and anxiety, and it can promote social support.

- Wood, A. M., Maltby, J., et al. (2008). The role of gratitude in the development of social support, stress, and depression: Two longitudinal studies. *Journal of Research in Personality,* 42(4): 854-871.

Oxytocin is a powerful neurotransmitter that is believed to influence social interactions and promote social bonds. Researchers found that variations in a certain gene can affect oxytocin secretion in the brain. The combination of oxytocin, genetics, and gratitude-related actions and feelings can play important roles in meaningful and significant relationships.

- Algoe, S. B. and Way, B. M. (2014). Evidence for a role of the oxytocin system, indexed by genetic variation in CD38, in the social bonding effects of expressed gratitude. *Social Cognitive and Affective Neuroscience,* 9(12): 1855-1861.

People can change their moods by using their memories. Remembering positive events or situations can increase the production of the feel-good chemical serotonin in the anterior cingulate cortex.

- Young, S. N. (2007). How to increase serotonin in the human brain without drugs. *Journal of Psychiatry & Neuroscience,* 32(6): 394-399.

Chapter 4

Courage vs. Fear

I had always thought that when I had grandchildren, I would want to live near them. But when I was working on my bachelor's degree as a 59-year-old in California, it wasn't in my plan to move to Oregon. That's where my pregnant daughter and her husband were working on *their* degrees.

I was overwhelmed thinking about leaving my family and friends. I would need to transfer my college credits to another university. Plus, I'd have to rent the other bedroom in my condo, and then find a room in someone else's home to save money. I was excited, anxious, and sad.

Still, the new-baby lure, plus the new information that I could graduate faster in Oregon, moved me forward.

I knew the importance of having a college degree, and I didn't want my daughter or her family to experience struggles similar to mine.

Still, I was concerned about myself. So I met with a trusted pastor and explained my situation.

After hearing the whole story, he agreed with my decision to move to Oregon. His suggestion was pivotal: Find scripture verses relating to courage and repeat them often. Then don't look back.

* * *

Within three years, there would be three graduations: my son-in-law's, mine, and my daughter's.

But before my daughter graduated, she had her second baby, and I would need to make another decision. Would I accept her invitation to move to Boston where my son-in-law had been accepted to graduate school?

Oh, that was easy. No way!!

I taught at a community college, and I did freelance writing for a medical center. Plus, I worked as a research assistant in a brain electrophysiology lab, aiming for a master's degree in neuropsychology.

Leave Oregon? You're kidding, right?!

But thoughts about my two grandkids, health issues of my daughter, eye surgery for my granddaughter, and the challenges of completing a graduate program with a baby *and* a preschooler – well, all that kept me thinking. And praying.

What was my purpose in life anyway? I was drawn to altruism, maybe for selfish reasons – such as love.

It seemed crucial to focus more on God. For weeks, I took prayer walks, talked to him, and repeated those courage-boosting scriptures. I needed time alone to think and pray. Then I decided.

On the nights that followed, I listened to one hymn over and over again: *Be Thou My Vision*. I needed God to lead me to a new city where I didn't know anyone and where I didn't have a job.

There was a reason for my solo trip. My daughter and her family would be stuck in Oregon until her husband's required summer classes ended in late August. One week later, graduate school was scheduled to begin in Boston. There wouldn't be enough time for them to move across the country and quickly find housing before school started.

We prayed and planned.

While still in Oregon, I would try to find a job and an apartment in Boston. Then I'd drive to Boston to help find housing for my daughter's family. After my son-in-law completed his classes, he and my daughter's father would drive a moving van to the East Coast and arrive just before the fall term began.

My daughter and her two little ones would travel by plane that same week. The timing would be tight, but this could work.

While in Oregon, I was thrilled when someone at a church helped me to quickly find a little room in Waltham, MA, to sublet for the summer. But I was having a hard time getting a job in Boston while I was sitting at my computer across the country.

Expecting to find a smaller apartment and higher rent, I sold my furniture. People helped me store boxes for the moving van, and they stuffed clothing and my computer into my car. Then I said goodbye to all the friends I'd made in Oregon.

My first stop was the Portland airport. I had arranged to meet my sister Dolores who was arriving from California to help with the first part of the drive. We'd stop in Michigan to see family. After that I'd travel alone – well, almost. I knew God was with me. Anxiety about work was buffered only when I thanked God *in advance* for what I believed he would do for me.

Approaching the Massachusetts state line, I received a call from a former client who I had been prospecting for work. He had just emailed a new contract and would be sending a retainer check.

Thank you, Lord!

But I didn't know how difficult it would be for us to overcome the next challenge: Find an affordable rental for a family that wasn't there to see it. And find that rental reasonably near the university – in one of the nation's most expensive areas.

I couldn't find it alone in Boston, and they couldn't find it alone in Oregon. We coordinated our search efforts. Much later, we would tally our emails to landlords and real estate agents. More than 350 contacts had been made.

As the date of their arrival approached, I was very worried. I hadn't found anything for my daughter's family, and my subletting arrangement would end soon. Where would I live? I hadn't even started looking for an apartment for myself.

Frequently when I couldn't sleep, I'd get out of bed and do something that a physician told me when I interviewed her for the *Los Angeles Times*.

In medical school, Shauna Blake Collins would often feel intense anxiety while trying to study. She would lie awake at night for hours with her books open, but she felt paralyzed by anxiety and couldn't study.

Everything changed after she heard a minister talk about getting rid of fear.

When she felt anxiety, she'd get out of bed and walk around her living room. Quietly, but audibly, she would pray. She'd repeatedly and firmly "tell the fear" to go away. Then she'd spend time thanking God in advance for the ability to study.

It was my understanding that by speaking this way and moving her body, she was redirecting electrical energy away from the amygdala. Also by expressing gratitude, she was affecting other brain areas associated with peace.

Anyway, I would copy her. After about 45 minutes, I'd usually get sleepy and go to bed. I figured that praying took a lot less time than worrying all night. But more important, I felt closer to God – and hopeful.

Some nights when my tough approach didn't work, I'd try my tender one – it was a tip from a trauma counselor. I would speak kindly to myself, reassuring myself as I would a little child. Then it was easier to imagine God's love and care.

As I looked for housing, I enjoyed networking with people, learning about Boston, and practicing a new accent.

Some people would be delightfully helpful. When I spoke with a patient realtor, she told me to *stop* trying to find an apartment for my family. Instead, find a house for all of us in an outlying area and sign the lease. That living arrangement was *definitely* not part of our plan, but under the circumstances, we agreed to adapt.

Someone else suggested checking the web-bulletin boards at churches.

When I called the woman who had advertised a beautiful three-story townhouse with a separate living area on the lower level, *and* a pond near the gardens outside, she asked, "What took you so long to call? The ad was up there for ten days."

Negotiations involved the whole search party and my daughter's dad. After the lease was signed and classes ended in Oregon, my daughter's family arrived just days before the new school term began.

Thank you, Power of our power.

Chapter 4: Courage vs. Fear

Scriptures and Affirmations

This is my command – be strong and courageous! Do not be afraid or discouraged. For the Lord your God is with you wherever you go. Joshua 1:9 (NLT)

- I AM strong and courageous.

I will make my people strong with power from me! They will go wherever they wish, and wherever they go, they will be under my personal care. Zechariah 10:12 (LB)

- I think of God's power making me strong. I receive his personal care, so I do what I need to do and go where I need to go.

God has given me power, love, and self-control. 2 Timothy. 1:7 (ESV)

- I believe that God has given me the power to think clearly, wisely, and lovingly. I can control myself.

Perfect love casts out fear. 1 John 4:18 (NKJV)

- I imagine that God loves me. I believe it. I speak and act lovingly to myself. I feel love for others.

When I am weak, then I am strong. 2 Corinthians 12:10 (NIV)

- When I feel weak, I imagine myself feeling strong from God's power.

Do not worry about tomorrow, for tomorrow will worry about itself. Each day has enough trouble of its own. Matthew 6:34 (NIV)

- I know that I can trust God to help me with the obstacles that I face today. Tomorrow, he'll help me again.

Do not be anxious for anything; but in everything, by prayer and petition, with thanksgiving, present your requests to God. Philippians 4:6 (NIV)

- I remember to ask God for what I need today. Then I thank him, even before my prayers are answered! If I worry again, I thank him again for his promised help.

No weapon turned against you shall succeed. Isaiah 54:17 (LB)

- I imagine that weapons like discouragement or fear will not succeed against me.

Do not be afraid or discouraged because of this vast army. For the battle is not yours, but God's. 2 Chronicles 20:15 (NIV)

- I am courageous. I imagine that I am not the only one fighting this battle. God is here, too. I am not discouraged or paralyzed by these problems. I can pray. I can think. I can take the next right step.

Let the peace of Christ rule your hearts, since as members of one body you were called to peace. Be thankful. Colossians 3:15 (NIV)

- I picture God's peace around me and inside me. I am grateful for the big things and the little things.

NOTES

Chapter 4: Courage vs. Fear

Related Science

Acute or chronic stress or anxiety can reduce the ability to solve problems and think creatively. In an experiment with 80 undergraduates, those who used self-affirmations showed an improvement in their problem-solving abilities.

- Creswell, J. D., Dutcher, J. M., et al. (2013). Self-affirmation improves problem-solving under stress. *PLOS One,* 8(5): e62593.

When a person makes an *effort* to overcome the fear of something, this effort causes activity in the brain region called the subgenual anterior cingulate cortex (sgACC). It's believed that the sgACC reduces the response to fear in other areas of the brain so that the person can act with courage.

- Nili, U., Goldberg, H., et al. (2010). Fear thou not: Activity of frontal and temporal circuits in moments of real-life courage. *Neuron,* 66(6): 949-962.

Chapter 5

Persistence vs. Quitting

Like many moms of her era, my mom had a favorite saying, "If at first you don't succeed, try, try again."

She raised five girls, including a set of twins and a daughter with brain damage. She worked in a dry cleaners, volunteered for civil rights projects, got a high-school equivalency certificate in her late 30s, and finally got a driver's license in her 40s. I know other people had greater challenges. Still, her work load was big.

When I was a teenager, she was preparing the upper level of our duplex to be a rental. She asked me and my 10-year-old sister to help her move a refrigerator up a flight of stairs.

"We can't do it, Ma. We gotta get some guys to help."

When necessary, she would flag down guys walking on our street and pay them a few dollars to help with heavy work. This was the 1960s.

"There aren't any guys around. We have to do it today!"

She needed the money. So we struggled.

When we were half-way up the stairs, the refrigerator got stuck.

"We CAN'T do this, Mom!

She yelled fiercely, *"I can do this!"* And with a bolt of energy, she shoved. It moved! She forced it up the stairs!

My mom had a habit that embarrassed me. She prayed out loud. But that afternoon, she had been swearing a lot in Serbian. Some people mockingly called her "Holy Mary." Still, she used her resources – God or adrenaline. In this case, adrenaline was pumping hard!

* * *

In unusual ways, my mom demanded persistence from us.

When a friend was driving me home one night, another driver ran a red light. He hit my side of the car, and my head slammed onto the dashboard. The result was partial amnesia.

70

The police drove me home. When the twins and Patty saw me, they were terrified. I didn't know the date or year. Memories of people and places were scrambled or non-existent.

"Do you remember me?"

"Rosie, what's my name?"

My mom was ticked and tired.

"What were you smoking?"

"Nothing!"

"What were you drinking?"

"Nothing!"

The police drove us to the hospital. After several hours, I was released from the emergency room, and I expected my mom to call a cab.

"We're walking!"

"But it's *one* in the morning! And it's freezing outside."

As we trudged along darkened streets, I tried to remember details of my life.

I'd ask her, "Is that right?"

"Wrong. Try again."

I tried to remember where I worked.

"Wrong. Try again."

My mom stayed awake with me as I drank tea and ate buttered saltines and tried to remember. She still had to get ready for work in a few hours.

Five days later, I was able to recall which buses would take me to my job. I'm not sure how productive I was when I arrived.

I attribute my fast recovery to my mom's persistence and my adrenaline from her abruptness. Maybe she hoped that walking in freezing temperatures would sharpen my wits. The prospect of having another daughter with a brain problem must have triggered every fear-it-fight-it circuit in *her* brain.

For a woman who boldly trusted God, I believe she might have been tapping into some deep wisdom.

* * *

Two decades after that incident, my mom and sister Patty moved to California. Patty lived in a nursing home about an hour from my mom's house. My mom wouldn't drive on the Los Angeles freeways, so my other sisters and I would take her to see Patty.

Although she visited Patty a couple times a week, she was determined to see her more often.

She began taking buses to the nursing home. The trip lasted a few hours. We were concerned about her, but when we learned more, we were shocked.

In the early evenings, she would transfer buses and wait alone on a street that was a couple blocks from Skid Row in downtown L.A.

Mom!!!!! Please, it's not safe!!!"

She said, "I am praying, and I know that my God is with me! I *will* be safe!"

Our pleading and arguing were useless. She was trusting God. And she persisted.

* * *

My mom *loved* the weather and foliage in Southern California. It was home for more than 25 years. After an illness, she went on hospice for a year. But the following year her condition improved, and she proudly "graduated."

I visited her on a beautiful summer day when she was in a small nursing home. She wanted to walk outside and smell the flowers, but the nurse explained that her muscles were too weak for her to walk. We would take her out in a wheelchair. The nurse and I left the room to talk about my mom's condition.

A little while later, we heard a loud thud. Running back into the room, we saw my mom slumped on the floor.

Looking like a sassy kid who got caught lighting a cigarette, she smirked, "I *like* taking risks!"

* * *

Learning math was difficult for me. In high school, I'd never taken algebra.

Instead, I took all the easiest classes, and I played drums in a band. I wanted music to be my career. One night, scouts from Motown Records watched our band perform. Our lead singer got a contract. Later, I would get a desk job with Motown in L.A. But that would happen years after a knee problem ended my career with other bands.

Before graduating from high school, a teacher gave me a last-minute suggestion: Go to college. I quickly applied to Wayne State University, got accepted, and received a grant for low-income students.

But I still didn't have study skills. So after a year, I quit. Nightmares of my failure and lost opportunities haunted me.

When I was 30, I had a major change in my life, and I shifted away from agnosticism and moved toward faith. I asked God for help and found a way to read difficult information. If my eyes drifted, or I was confused, I'd point to the words, pause briefly, and picture their meaning.

This new ability inspired hope that I could have a meaningful career. I read *What Color Is Your Parachute?* and learned I had the qualities of a writer and teacher – even though I didn't have the skills. The author wrote that skills could be learned. So I studied grammar books for third graders, writing books for teens, and textbooks for journalists. Eventually, I wrote self-help articles for the *San Bernardino Sun*.

By my mid-40s, I was a divorced mom with two daughters, and I *really* needed to earn money. I wrote radio commercials for a couple of years, and then found a short assignment with Loma Linda University Medical Center. I'd be interviewing nutrition experts and a department head from Harvard. This was definitely out of my league.

The editor had confidence in me, but when I finally received the preparatory background material, I panicked. The science research was dense and detailed.

As I drove to Loma Linda, I repeated an encouraging sentence from the Bible for the two-hour drive. When I arrived, I felt calm and confident. I really believed what

I'd been saying: I can do all things through Christ who strengthens me. And I felt the peaceful companionship of God.

The assignment went well, and I later signed a contract to write a weekly health and nutrition column for the university. Understanding science became easier on the days that I relied on God. That meant chatting with him.

"So Lord, what do you think I should do here?"

I'd breathe to relax, write my concerns, and then list possible solutions. I never heard a voice that said, "DO THIS!" Sometimes I'd get a great idea, and I'd thank God. Other times, I'd make the most logical choice. When I was on a deadline, I couldn't sit around and meditate.

To meet other writers, I organized a small group of journalists who were Christians. They encouraged me to write for the *Los Angeles Times* and go back to school.

I finally signed up for that algebra class that I'd been avoiding for decades. To decrease my fear of math, I would force myself to smile, dance around the house, and say, "I love math. This is going to be great! I *can* do this!

The class required a lot of work, but I did well. Because the concepts were so difficult for me, I took some tests to assess my learning abilities.

When I finished, the test administrator brought the program director into the room. They looked concerned.

"Are you partially blind?"

"What?!! "No, I'm not."

I'd scored well on the language and reading portions of the test, but I bombed the visual section. Although my first five answers were correct, I didn't have sufficient time to answer the next 25 questions.

I was so discouraged that I didn't continue the testing. But later, I created drills to help me improve my short-term memory and my ability to quickly translate images into words.

As I learned more about neuroscience, study strategies, and the effect of stress on the brain, my courses became easier. At age 61, I was grateful to God when I finally graduated – and with honors.

Other people face similar challenges. In Boston, I had the opportunity to share what I'd learned with low-income students who had experienced trauma. So they could pass their high school equivalency tests, I taught writing skills, study strategies, and reading comprehension.

Sometimes, I think that I overcame these obstacles by myself. But when I take time to remember the depth of

God's help, I feel as if I've dropped the weight of pride off my shoulders. It seems like a sunny day, birds are chirping, and I'm gently swaying in a hammock between two palm trees.

Chapter 5: Persistence vs. Quitting

Scriptures and Affirmations

Not by might, not by power, but by my Spirit, says the Lord of Hosts. You will succeed because of my Spirit, though you are few and weak. Zechariah 4:6 (LB)

- I choose to believe that God will help me to succeed even when I'm alone and weak. I envision that he will provide what I need.

I can do all things through him who gives me strength. Philippians 4:12 (NIV)

- I CAN do all things through Christ who strengthens me. I imagine getting help from God and completing my goals.

Since we are surrounded by such a great cloud of witnesses, let us throw off everything that hinders and the sin that so easily entangles, and let us run with perseverance the race marked out for us. Hebrews 12:1 (NIV)

- I envision persisting and achieving my purpose in life. I ignore distractions and things that throw me off my course.

I will strengthen them in the Lord and in his name they will walk. Zechariah 10:12 (NIV)

- I believe that God is making me strong with his power.

Fight the good fight of faith.1 Timothy 6:12 (NIV)

- I imagine overcoming the obstacles that I will face today. I fight fear with faith.

Let us hold unswervingly to the hope we profess, for he who promised is faithful. Hebrews 10:23 (NIV)

- I utterly believe that God will help me persist to achieve the things that are good for me.

In every battle you will need faith as your shield to stop the fiery arrows aimed at you by Satan. Ephesians 6:16 (LB)

- I imagine that God is my shield, and he helps me overcome problems.

God, with his mercy, gave us this work to do. So we don't give up! 2 Corinthians 4:16 (ICB)

- I see myself persisting and firmly refusing to quit. I get moving.

Let us not become weary in doing good, for at the proper time we will reap a harvest if we do not give up. Galatians 6:9 (NIV)

- I refuse to quit. I believe that there will be a payoff for my hard work and doing the right things.

You have begun to live the new life, in which you are being made new and are becoming like the One who made you. This new life brings you the true knowledge of God. Colossians 3:10 (NCV)

- I am choosing to renew my mind with positive words, thoughts, and behaviors.

NOTES

Chapter 5: Persistence vs. Quitting

Related Science

Doing activities related to long-term goals produces activity in the prefrontal cortex and releases good-feeling dopamine in the nucleus accumbens.

- Goto, Y. and Grace, A. A. (2005). Dopaminergic modulation of limbic and cortical drive of nucleus accumbens in goal-directed behavior. *Nature Neuroscience,* 8(6): 805-812.

Dopamine levels help to regulate motivation to do positive activities. But for some people who are sensation seekers, dopamine can regulate motivation to do negative activities.

- Salamone, J. D. and Correa, M. (2012). The mysterious motivational functions of mesolimbic dopamine. *Neuron,* 76(3): 470-485.

Some people expect future positive events even though there is no likelihood that those events will occur. The tendency toward optimism is related to activity in the rostral anterior cingulate cortex. This study showed that the brain can produce the *tendency* to expect positive events or experiences.

- Sharot, T., Riccardi, A. M., et al. (2007). Neural mechanisms mediating optimism bias. *Nature.* doi:10.1038/nature06280

Chapter 6

Self-forgiveness vs. Shame

I know we've all done embarrassing things. I've done a lot of them – especially during my 20s.

I'm not going to talk much about the night I went out dancing and woke up in the morning with an inflated ego. Then one of my friends invited me to an audition for dancers at the Burbank movie studios. Oh, she *knew* we'd get picked because she had friends in show business!

I was OK with the jazz-dance segment, but I won't go into detail about how I tried to tap dance *without* tap shoes and *without* ever having taken a tap dancing lesson.

No, I won't talk much about the movie people who covered their laughing mouths and the 200-plus *real* dancers who were probably snickering as I did my rendition of tap dancing while making big circles with my arms like a three-year-old.

And I'll just hint about the puny and fumbling basketball team I organized in Hollywood. Many of the women had never played team sports. We were always losing. But before playing the best team in the league, we giddily pumped up our bravado, *promised* to focus on the ball, and won the game.

Instead of a story that I eventually laughed about, I'll share an embarrassing story about misplaced trust and neuroplasticity, and later finding hope.

* * *

When I was 21, I was looking for a way to resolve anxiety and depression. After reading a popular book about a new therapy promoted by celebrities, I signed up and went to Los Angeles.

The six-month program was gradually extended. Over time, close friendships were formed. Eventually, the organization was restructured into a community. Many people enjoyed the social life – parties, team sports, and traveling together. As positive publicity increased, so did the popularity. And so did the profits. But after nine years, major problems surfaced.

November 4, 1980, Election Day. While I was in a weekly meeting with about 20 people, I heard serious accusations about finances, ethics, and cruelty. People were furious about the sexual misconduct of a therapist.

Listening to the details, I was stunned. And then I thought, "He's just a man. We've made him a god!"

Exposed lies shattered the idealistic "truth" that glued the community together.

The next day, I was upset to hear that other therapists involved in ethics violations simply wanted to change the leadership and had arranged a meeting for the 350 community members. I wasn't a journalist then, but I called the *Los Angeles Times* to send a reporter. No one was available.

So seven men and I interrupted the meeting to tell the truth. We had decided earlier that I would speak since I was one of the most long-term members. And most likely, people would believe me. I told people about the initial goodwill of some therapists, the promises for a better life, and the benefits I'd received. I explained how the organization had evolved, and how manipulation, pressure, and extremism grew.

"It's all over. It's time to go home."

It had been only 24 hours since a small group of fed-up people banded together, found support, and elected to confront a mini-god.

In the next 24 hours, a friend and I left the community and rented a business associate's vacant house. Although it had spectacular hilltop views, the house was isolated. And so was I.

The combined abrupt changes had a physical and emotional effect on me. My physician suggested that I organize a meeting with group members and the head of the Neuropsychiatric Institute at UCLA. Dr. Louis West gave his assessment to the group: We had been in a cult.

Looking back, I would deeply regret times of not trusting my intuition, not asking questions, not listening carefully, and not keeping my faith.

Instead, I trusted authority figures who believed their own lies. When the attorney for the plaintiffs heard about my talk to community members, he asked me to testify. I declined. When a defendant asked me to testify, I declined. I had to think about this mess without pressure or outside influences.

Ultimately, many of the therapists at the Center for Feeling Therapy would lose their licenses to practice.

In the confusing aftermath, I looked for answers. How could this have happened in a group where the members included physicians, lawyers, accountants, and educators?

I could only speak for myself. In the beginning, I had asked questions about the promised benefits, but the answers were vague or distracting. I dismissed my concerns and trusted authority figures who appeared knowledgeable.

Telling my life stories to a compassionate and supportive therapist had boosted my esteem. Expressing emotions had been empowering. But I had ignored my nagging conscience about blaming people for my problems.

I had adapted to hearing sarcasm from some therapists. Much later in the organization, when I saw ethical violations and asked questions about them, excuses were made by the therapists.

"This is an *innovative community*, an *experimental community*, not traditional therapy."

That answer had given the impression of specialness and immunity. Although confused, I had accepted the excuse.

Even though I had worked, played, and dated outside the community for many years, I had believed warnings that life outside the community would be a big mistake.

At the end of a long and difficult self-assessment, I learned two main important lessons.

First, by not thinking critically about what I heard and saw, I – and many others – had inadvertently empowered people who misused their influence and credentials.

Second, I learned that fear or personal needs can silence a person. So can the loss of benefits. Smart people can act like they're ignorant. Observant people can act like they're blind. We're born with an Achilles' heel. And it can get weaker when people have strong emotions or when they stop reasoning.

In other realms, a similar process is called "groupthink." Scholars explain that it happens when members of tight in-groups strive for unity, but they ignore intuition, suppress dissent, isolate themselves, and fail to realistically assess situations. The outcome is irrational thinking and poor decision-making.

The process was linked to NASA's role in the Challenger Space Shuttle explosion, President Kennedy's decision to invade Cuba, and other disasters or fiascos involving intelligent, successful people.

After the fallout, news stories troubled me. Although some people truly reported bizarre experiences, those experiences were not mine, nor were they the experiences of many other people in the organization.

I was concerned that the public would not be informed of the *common* traps that caught people like me and could catch others. They were *thinking* traps.

For me, that was the big news story that could protect and empower readers.

I later learned that those traps had a name: "logical fallacies." They were the half-truths and the emotional appeals that triggered fear or false hope. They were the generalizations, sarcastic comments, and distractions from important questions. They were the outright lies and subtle manipulations that had cost me money and nine years. But I, along with hundreds of people, had jumped on the bandwagon. And my knees were skinned. I had fallen on the dark side of neuroplasticity. When I stood up again, I knew the dangers of not thinking critically.

* * *

After I left the community, I was intensely cynical. Eventually, I felt the need to believe in *something*. I evaluated my options. Buddhism, New Age, Judaism, Jesus? I decided to try God.

I talked to him, but not in a religious way. I swore a lot about people who had upset me. Surprisingly, the venting made me feel closer to him. After a while, I cleaned up my language and told him deep truths about myself.

I began going into empty churches. Then full churches. But the strongest connection to God came when I walked and silently talked to him. I focused on the trees, sky, and flowers. I associated the beauty and ruggedness with God's goodness, kindness, and strength. Feeling gratitude toward God was healing.

These walks and talks cleared my mind of anxiety, anger, and regret. They became a habit and a life changer. On one of them, I chose to follow the teachings of Jesus.

That created a new problem. Television evangelist Jim Bakker was in the news at that time. A multitude of believers supported his blatantly lavish lifestyle. He was later convicted of conspiracy and fraud. That sounded too familiar.

There was a warning sign in my brain. Was this another example of group dynamics gone awry? Did strong emotions – or passion for a cause – subdue reasoning, dull intuition, influence decisions, or silence insiders?

I was concerned. Could my new trust in God be transferred inadvertently to a person who was manipulative, dishonest, or did not share my values?

How could someone or something thwart the normal lie detectors in my brain?

I knew the answer. I would stay aware of those thinking traps and clever distractions that I had ignored in the past. I felt supported when I found a directive in the Bible – love God with your heart, soul, *mind*, and body. That meant God wanted people to think.

Sometimes in churches I heard messages that didn't make sense to me. The wrathful scriptures made me anxious or angry. Various pastors had various answers to questions. When I told a pastor that I didn't believe his answer, he told me to ask God. Hmmm. I liked that.

In the meantime, I focused on scriptures that gave me peace and acknowledged the ones that revealed my weak spots. I would *try* to be Christ-like.

These days, I'm conscious when people in the news, trendsetters, and even ministers belittle reasoning or use logical fallacies. I sometimes pray and bless them with balance, humility, or truth. That helps me maintain my awareness, yet feel compassion or see my weaknesses. It also inspires action and hope.

* * *

I once learned an eloquent lesson from a woman who had been a migrant farm worker. Her son Joel Ramirez was graduating from medical school at UCLA. I introduced myself as a reporter doing a story for the *L.A. Times* about neuroscience.

The mother tilted her head and raised her hand to stop me from speaking.

In accented English, she said, "Excuse me, what is neuroscience?"

I was surprised by her question. Then I explained.

After the interview, I kept mulling over what had happened. First, I felt bad for speaking quickly and unintentionally using a word she may not have understood.

Second, there were TV cameras and lots of media people near us on the campus. Having limited English, she could have felt intimidated talking to a journalist. But she appeared to have enough self-assurance, humility, or honesty to stop me and ask for clarification.

She said she always wanted to be a teacher. She was mine.

* * *

While teaching in Oregon, I had a problem with a college student. After she spoke with the dean about some disruptive behavior, she was allowed to return to class. I wondered how she would act and how the other students would respond to her.

On the first day when she walked back into the room, she smiled, stretched out her arms, and shouted, "IT'S A NEW DAY!"

Wow, what a role model for moving forward in life!

Chapter 6: Self-forgiveness vs. Shame

Scriptures and Affirmations

You will again have compassion on us; you will tread our sins underfoot and hurl all our iniquities into the depths of the sea. Micah 7:19 (NIV)

- I picture God having compassion for me. I envision him throwing away my sins. I believe they're gone, and so is guilt!

All have sinned; all fall short of God's glorious ideal; yet now God declares us "not guilty" of offending him if we trust in Jesus Christ, who in his kindness freely takes away our sins. Romans 3:23 (LB)

- I think about Jesus forgiving me. I trust him to do it. So I am forgiven. And I forgive myself.

If we confess our sins, he is faithful and just, and will forgive us our sins and purify us from all unrighteousness. 1 John 1:9 (NIV)

- I tell Jesus about the things I've done wrong, and remember that he always forgives me. I refuse to have that haunting feeling of shame.

I've blotted out your sins; they're gone like morning mist at noon! Isaiah 44:22 (LB)

- I believe that God removes guilt and shame. They vanish, just like fog vanishes.

Their sins and lawless acts I will remember no more. And where these have been forgiven, there is no longer any sacrifice for sin. Hebrews 10:17 (NIV)

- I believe that God forgives my mistakes after I confess them to him. I don't need to feel guilty, anxious, or depressed.

There was a time when some of you were just like that, but now your sins are washed away, and you are set apart for God. He has accepted you because of what the Lord Jesus Christ and the Spirit of our God have done for you. 1 Corinthians 6:11 (LB)

- I imagine that my sins are washed away. I believe that He accepts me because of what Jesus has done for me.

Who dares accuse us whom God has chosen as his own? Will God? No! He is the one who has forgiven us and given us right standing with himself. Who then will condemn us? Will Christ? No! For he is the one who died for us and came back to life again for us and is sitting at the place of highest honor next to God, pleading for us there in heaven. Romans 8:33 (LB)

- I imagine God forgiving me. I imagine ignoring false accusations and negative memories. I think about Jesus accepting me and loving me.

Everyone who trusts in Jesus is freed from all guilt and declared righteous. Acts 13:39 (LB)

- I trust in Jesus, so I'm freed from guilt!

NOTES

Chapter 6: Self-forgiveness vs. Shame

Related Science

Simply choosing to have an attitude of forgiveness, instead of an unforgiving one, has a positive impact on the central and peripheral nervous systems. The forgiving attitude promotes psychological and physical health.

- Worthington, E. L., Jr., Witvliet, C. V., et al. (2007). Forgiveness, health, and well-being: A review of evidence for emotional versus decisional forgiveness, dispositional forgivingness, and reduced unforgiveness. *Journal of Behavioral Health,* 30(4): 291-302.

Research showed that regretting life choices can motivate goal setting, but regret does not necessarily result in achieving those goals. Women who made life changes based on their new goals reported having more well-being than those who did not.

- Stewart, A. J. and Vandewater, E. A. (1999). "If I had it to do over again...": Midlife review, midcourse corrections, and women's well-being in midlife. *Journal of Personality and Social Psychology* 76(2): 270-283.

Research can help people to understand the power of social relationships and communities. Psychologists studied people who lived in the slums of Calcutta. They found that strong social relationships were credited with satisfaction in specific life areas, even though the overall satisfaction with life was generally poor.

- Biswas-Diener, R. and Diener, E. (2001). Making the best of a bad situation: Satisfaction in the slums of Calcutta. *Social Indicators Research,* 55(3): 329-352.

Emotions can be transferred to other people and spread through social groups. However, some people are more susceptible than others to contagious emotion and messages.

- Ilies, R., Wagner, D. T., et al. (2007). Explaining affective linkages in teams: Individual differences in susceptibility to contagion and individualism–collectivism. *Journal of Applied Psychology,* 92(4): 1140-1148.

Chapter 7

Healing vs. Pain

I re-read the question on the dental consent form: Do you have temporomandibular joint disorder (TMJ)? No. I hadn't been bothered by it in almost 20 years. So I didn't have it anymore. Right?

After the dental work was finished and the anesthetic wore off, the pain in my face was horrible. It continued for months. I saw three specialists, used a mouthpiece, and followed the dentist's directions. Still, pain.

One morning at 2:00 a.m., I thought I couldn't tolerate the pain anymore. I crawled out of bed and onto the floor. I had to talk to someone. I remembered watching a Christian TV program and seeing a phone number to call for prayer. I'd scoffed at healings by TV evangelists, but now I was desperate.

I called the number. As I waited to talk to someone, a recording played Bible verses. I was irritated. More tension. More pain.

But instinctively, I knew I had to make a decision, a choice to believe. I started repeating the scriptures that I heard, and I forced out my skeptical thoughts.

Minutes later, a man came on the phone line. Without an introduction, I continued praying, "I believe that God can stop this pain in my face and jaw...." The man prayed with me.

After twenty minutes, I realized the pain was gone. We thanked God, and I got off the phone. Then I wrote down exactly what had happened. I slept well for the first time in months.

The next morning, I immediately read and re-wrote my notes. It seemed crucial to continue thanking God. I intuitively knew that I needed to avoid looking for the pain, or trying to recall it.

When the creeping pain twinges triggered worries, I forced myself to smile and thank God again for healing me. I repeatedly spoke the Bible verses. I distracted myself and *refused* to focus on the pain.

Three months later, TMJ specialist David Shirazi took new images of my jaw. When he re-entered the room, he was excited.

"You came in here with degeneration of your condyle jaw bone. These images show that you have new bone growth."

During my initial visit, Shirazi had explained there was a small chance that new bone growth might occur with his treatment. I was thrilled about this success.

I don't know exactly when that new bone growth began, but I *absolutely* know that the pain had stopped twenty minutes after I made the *choice* to believe that God could heal me, and I *repeated* those scripture verses about healing.

* * *

At one time in my life when I had intense anxiety, typical prayers weren't working. A visiting minister, well known for healing, suggested something I'd never heard before.

"Pick five scriptures about overcoming fear and say them aloud three times a day. Do it for a week, and then call me if necessary."

It wasn't. I was on the road to feeling better.

Someone later asked me, "Were you trusting God to change circumstances or were you trusting yourself?"

Trusting God. He gave me a brain and scriptures to *use* to improve my health, change my circumstances, and transform my life.

"Is this some new style of prayer?"

It might be an ancient one.

Early Christians who didn't read or write must have memorized Jesus' words by saying them repeatedly as they walked around or did their work. It seems to have changed their lives.

Chapter 7: Healing vs. Pain

Scriptures and Affirmations

Your faith has healed you. Go in peace and be freed from your suffering. Mark 5:34 (NIV)

- I have faith in Jesus, and he heals me. I am being set free from pain. I choose to think peaceful, calming thoughts. I think about Jesus' love and how he heals people.

A cheerful heart is good like medicine. Proverbs 17:22 (LB)

- I smile and speak cheerfully because I know it's like medicine. I believe it helps to heal me. I take a big dose of cheerfulness several times a day.

I will restore you to health and heal your wounds. Jeremiah 30:17 (NIV)

- I believe that God heals illnesses and injuries. He restores my health. I can relax and trust him and thank him in advance for that healing.

Pleasant sights and good reports give happiness and health. Proverbs 15:30 (LB)

- I take time to enjoy nature, or pictures of it. I share uplifting stories and encouraging news. I avoid talking needlessly about pain or trying to remember how bad I felt.

I tell you the truth, whatever you bind on earth will be bound in heaven, and whatever you loose on earth will be loosed in heaven. Matthew 18:18 (NIV)

- I tell this pain to stop! I firmly refuse to focus on pain. Instead, I focus on God's power, on how he's helped me in the past, and on how I will feel when he heals me again. I tell my body to get well.

Your own soul is nourished when you are kind; it is destroyed when you are cruel. Proverbs 11:17 (LB)

- I'm kind to myself and others. Kindness nourishes my soul, my mind, and my body. I refuse to be mean to myself or others.

Whatever is true, whatever is noble, whatever is right, whatever is pure, whatever is lovely, whatever is admirable — if anything is excellent or praiseworthy — think about such things. Philippians 4:8 (NIV)

- I think and talk about things that are good, lovely, and admirable, especially when I'm in pain. I think about things that I *can* do. I avoid thinking about things I can't do. Even before the pain stops, I thank God for healing me.

Speak to these bones for me. Tell them, "Dry bones, listen to the word of the Lord! This is what the Lord God says to you: I will cause breath to come into you, and you will come to life!" Ezekiel 37:4 (ERV)

- I breathe deeply to help heal my body. I imagine that the pain is dissolved and exhaled from my body.

Gentle words cause life and health. Proverbs 15:4 (LB)

- I speak tenderly to myself when I'm sick. I tell my body to get well. But I firmly tell illness to go away. Gentleness to myself and others makes me feel loved. And it sweetly moves me forward when I feel discouraged.

If the Spirit of him who raised Jesus from the dead is living in you, he who raised Christ from the dead will also give life to your mortal bodies.... Romans 8:11 (NIV)

- If the Holy Spirit can raise Jesus from the dead, then he can make me well! He can reduce this pain and distract me from it.

NOTES

Chapter 7: Healing vs. Pain

Related Science

Along with physical and psychological factors, our expectations and beliefs play a role in how much pain we feel.

- Wagner, T. D., Riling, J. K., et al. (2004). Placebo-induced changes in fMRI in the anticipation and experience of pain. *Science*, 303(5661): 1162-1167.

Anxiety can increase the perception of chronic pain. And it works the other way around. Chronic pain can increase anxiety. Research suggests that a process occurring in neurons in the anterior cingulate cortex, an important area for pain perception, plays a special role in chronic pain and the anxiety related to it.

- Zhuo, M. (2016). Neural mechanisms underlying anxiety-chronic pain interactions. Trends in *Neurosciences*, 39(3): 136-145.

Self-affirmations cause activity in the powerful reward centers of the brain – the ventral striatum and ventromedial prefrontal cortex. Plus, these same brain areas help to reduce pain. Also, they help us act in a stable way when we're threatened.

Other areas of the brain – the medial prefrontal cortex and the posterior cingulate – are affected by self-affirmations. These areas act like shock absorbers for threatening information.

- Cascio, C. N., O'Donnell, M. B., et al. (2016). Self-affirmation activates brain systems associated with self-related processing and reward and is reinforced by future orientation. *Social Cognitive and Affective Neuroscience,* 11(4): 621-629.

Chapter 8

Comfort vs. Loneliness

About two months after leaving Boston and relocating to the small town of Saline, Michigan, I did something I knew was wrong.

I worked far beyond my physical limits and then did errands. Later that night, I took a walk and was too tired to re-tie my shoestring. When I stumbled and hit the sidewalk, I knew I'd broken my knee.

As I waited in the emergency room with my daughter, I managed the pain with prayer and deep breathing. During the whole recovery time, I needed only three tablets of ibuprofen. After two months, I was walking without a leg brace.

On the tenth week of my recovery, it was December 21, the longest and darkest night of the year. The holiday is called Yalda Night in Iran and several Central Asian countries.

In Iranian communities around Los Angeles and other cities, friends gather to spend the dark night together, laughing and eating foods that remind them that brighter days are coming. In years long past, I had celebrated Yalda with my friend Homa, who was from Tehran.

Later that night, one of my sisters called me. Our conversation drifted toward a time when we weren't close. She asked me to talk about that. I briefly explained, and she kindly apologized. She asked about other instances.

"I really shouldn't talk anymore about it. Discussing it will only open a can of worms."

Years earlier, my older sister Kris had given me a wonderful lesson on forgiveness.

"Honey, don't go back and review all the arguments. Just forgive each other for what the person did and forgive yourself for what you may have done. Start all over now."

When my younger sister asked again about the past issues, my intuition said, "Don't explain." Instead, I explained. I spoke carefully. Fortunately, I had to end the call and finish my errands.

But the conversation didn't stop there. I had lit a fire in my brain. The more I recalled, the more I seethed. The more I felt self-righteous, the more I ignored memories of times I had offended her.

I planned what I'd do: I'd go home, eat dinner, call my sister, and let her know what I was *really* thinking. In couched terms, of course.

When I was standing in my kitchen – *simply standing* – the top of my leg suddenly slid backward and the bottom part of my leg slid forward. I hit the floor. The pain was excruciating.

The emergency room nurse gave me instructions and suggested that I stay home (they were swamped). I should see my orthopedist in the morning. Neighbors and my daughter stopped by to help.

Unlike the night when I'd broken my kneecap, I couldn't manage this pain. I had a hard time regulating my breathing. I couldn't sleep. I could barely pray. I was alone.

I kept thinking that by rehearsing vengeance for so long, I had caused adrenaline to flood through my body. I was ready for an attack – but the attack backfired.

It was the longest night of the year.

The next day, the orthopedist saw my melon-sized knee and explained that the severe buckling probably occurred because my muscles were still weak.

During the days, I'd do freelance writing and search online for more work. During the nights, I'd lie in bed feeling depressed and isolated in this new town.

I imagined what it would be like to be sick, old, and regretful in a nursing home, not having accomplished my goals. Between the depressing thoughts, the pain, and the insomnia, it was hard to think that God was with me or to feel his love.

I remembered feeling this lonely at another time in my life. Then, I'd visit older people who seemed lonely too. I'd bring them food, or I'd call to check in. I also recalled visiting my sister Patty in nursing homes, and how those visits made her happy and made me feel more loving and less lonely. So I prayed to meet an older woman who needed a friend.

Awhile later, I was hobbling in a store and an elderly British woman started a conversation with me. Then she invited me to her home for tea. During the following months, she initiated our visits, helped me get adjusted to the new town, and called to just check-in.

She was the friendly visitor I had hoped I could be to someone who needed a friend. She was a gift – God's love with an English accent.

That winter, I couldn't take long walks. So I'd open my curtains and pray as I looked at the snow, stars, fog, or barren trees. I was connecting to the Gift Giver.

Chapter 8: Comfort vs. Loneliness

Scriptures and Affirmations

Come near to God and he will come near to you. James 4:8 (NIV)

- I talk with God and write to him. I think about God being close to me in my home, in my car, and in my office. I believe that God is near me.

Though my father and mother forsake me, the Lord will receive me. Psalms 27:10 (NIV)

- I know that God never abandons me. Even if my family or friends left me, God would welcome me and comfort me.

God, in his holy dwelling, is a father to orphans and defender of widows. Psalm 68:5 (CSB)

- I imagine that God is with me. When I feel lonely or upset, I think about him helping me, directing me, or defending me.

You can pray for anything, and if you believe, you have it; it's yours! But when you are praying, first forgive anyone you are holding a grudge against, so that your Father in heaven will forgive your sins too. Mark 11:24 (LB)

- I forgive people who hurt me – I know I've hurt other people, too. I can trust God to provide me with the things that I need.

NOTES

Chapter 8: Comfort vs. Loneliness

Related Science

A comprehensive analysis of 148 research studies and more than 308,000 participants showed having strong social connections helped people to *survive* health problems. However, without social connections there is an *increased risk* for health problems.

- Holt-Lunstad, J., Smith, T. B., et al. (2010). Social relationships and mortality risk: A meta-analytic review. *PLOS Medicine,*
  doi.org/10.1371/journal.pmed.1000316.

For older people, volunteering for religious causes was shown to improve mental health more than volunteering for secular organizations or causes.

- Musick, M. A. and Wilson, J. (2003). Volunteering and depression: The role of psychological and social resource in different age groups. *Social Science & Medicine,* 56(2): 259-269.

This study involved 1,200 older adults in two different cultures. In Spain, many older people provide and receive *instrumental* support. For example, help with housekeeping, finances, and transportation. This was shown to be protective against loneliness.

But in Northern Europe where independence is highly valued, a different pattern was found. Older people provided and received more *emotional* support. When emotional support was received, it was protective against loneliness.

- Sanchez Rodrigues, M. M., De Jong Gierveld, J., et al. (2014). Loneliness and the exchange of social support among older adults in Spain and the Netherlands. *Aging and Society,* 34(2): 330-354.

Chapter 9

Rest vs. Overwork

With five kids, my mom always had plenty to do. But on Sundays, she would say, "No hard work!"

That meant, after church we would help prepare meals and wash dishes. Then we could watch movies, play board games, go outside, read, or visit. Sundays were my respite from housework and schoolwork.

Years passed. I forgot those habits and sometimes worked every day of the week. In my thirties, a co-worker who was Jewish told me she spent the Sabbath relaxing, reading, eating, and visiting. I was so jealous!

I wondered why I didn't think I should do that, too. I had the same Ten Directives: No murder, no stealing, no lying, etc. Why was it OK to eliminate the most fun one? Rest on Sunday!

Gradually, I wove rest into my Sundays. As a married mom with two little girls, I found ways to reduce the work load. I'd cook extra food on Saturday, serve simple meals on Sundays, and plan to work or shop on the other days.

Some of the best Sundays were when my family and I would go to the Santa Monica Mountains. My husband would notice families who were "doing it right."

They'd bring lots of food, play games, listen to music, and stay at the park all day – not just a couple hours like we did. I wanted to do that, too.

As a busy single mom, I went to the mountains less often with my girls, and my day of rest might start on Friday night, Saturday, or Sunday.

Years later, my adult daughter would ask me what I wanted to do for my birthday. The answer was always the same: Let's have a picnic!

This year when she asked, I told her I wanted an *all-day* picnic. With her, my son-in-law, and my three grandchildren, we spent *seven* whole hours on Sunday relaxing by a lake, eating, napping, talking, and laughing. We got it right!

That night, I was so happy that I could barely fall asleep. I kept thanking God for a full day of rest with my loved ones while basking in the beauty of his nature.

Chapter 9: Rest vs. Overwork

Scriptures and Affirmations

It is useless for you to work so hard from early morning until late at night, anxiously working for food to eat; for God gives rest to his loved ones. Psalm 127:2 (NLT)

- I take short breaks during my workday, and I rest in the evening. I work calmly, take care of problems, and refuse to worry. I know that God will help me rest at night.

My presence will go with you, and I will give you rest. Exodus 33:14 (NIV)

- I picture God with me as I rest. He will help me sleep.

Come to me, all you who are weary and burdened, and I will give you rest. Take my yoke upon you and learn from me, for I am gentle and humble in heart, and you will find rest for your souls. For my yoke is easy and my burden is light. Matthew 11:28 (NIV)

- I imagine giving Jesus my worries and problems. I trust that he will help me to be gentle and honest with myself. That helps me to rest.

I lay down and slept in peace and woke up safely, for the Lord was watching over me. Psalms 3:5 (NIV)

- I think about God watching over me as I lie down to sleep. I tell myself that I can sleep peacefully and safely because God cares for me.

Rest in the Lord; wait patiently for him to act. Psalms 37:7 (LB)

- I breathe deeply as I imagine Jesus, and I rest. I trust him to help me with my problems.

NOTES

Chapter 9: Rest vs. Overwork

Related Science

Deep breathing, or diaphragmatic breathing, can significantly reduce cortisol and stress. In addition, it can improve the ability to pay attention and focus.

- Xiao Ma, Zi-Qi Yue, et al. (2017). The effect of diaphragmatic breathing on attention, negative affect and stress in healthy adults. *Frontiers in Psychology*, 8: 874.
  doi: 10.3389/fpsyg.2017.00874

Learning and new memories are consolidated in the hippocampus, and that brain area functions best only when a person has a full night's sleep.

- Yoo, S. S., Hu, P. T., et al. (2007). A deficit in the ability to form new human memories without sleep. *Nature Neuroscience*, 10(3): 385-392.

Working long hours may have a negative effect on memory and reasoning abilities. In a study of more than 2,000 participants, researchers found that working 55 hours or more per week was associated with lower scores on a vocabulary test, and it reduced abilities on a reasoning test.

- Virtanen, M., Singh-Manoux A., et al. (2009). Long working hours and cognitive function: The Whitehall II Study. *American Journal of Epidemiology,* 169(5): 596-605.

During an experiment done by the Boston Consulting Group, consultants found that professionals who had a strict system of taking evenings off and one day off each week had more positive perceptions of their work circumstances than their peers who were not in the experiment.

The participants also had increased learning, development, open communication, and a better product for their clients. As part of the experiment, the consultants encouraged dialogue among all the participants and insisted on leadership support.

- Perlow, L. A. and Porter, J. L. (2009). Making time off predictable – and required. *Harvard Business Review*. Retrieved on 10/18/17 from https://hbr.org/2009/10/making-time-off-predictable-and-required

Epilogue

Hope

Neuroscientist Eric Kandel told me that all living things require hope for survival. But sometimes we hope and pray, and prayers don't get answered.

My sister Patty died of complications related to un-shunted hydrocephalus. My marriage ended. And my eldest daughter ignored my worries and went on a world-wide trip, for the most part – alone.

But on her first day in Beijing, a *different prayer was answered*. She met a great guy. And he happened to be from Colorado. They traveled together, returned to the U.S. for several years, and recently eloped to Copenhagen. A few days ago, I went to Los Angeles for their wedding reception.

As I waited outside the airport terminal for my ride, I recalled other arrivals and departures here. The sights and smells triggered a flood of emotions – joy, love, laughter, bliss, disgust, longing, sadness, and grief. They were the emotions of nearly four decades of my life.

I had to re-organize myself. I chose to use gratitude. I thanked God for all the blessings and all the life I had experienced here, for all the people who had been a special part of my life, and for all the breath-taking gifts of nature. As I did that, the mist of sadness disappeared. Gratitude gently turned into hope.

Here's a parting message for you, dear reader. Keep hope alive – for something, for anything. Hope feels better than despair. And gratitude to God can feel the best.

Rosie Clandos

November 4, 2017

Postscript

In 1876, Scottish author, poet, and minister George MacDonald wrote a parting message that still applies today. In Michael Phillips' translation of MacDonald's novel, *The Curate's Awakening*, a woman asks a minister to teach her to believe. He tells her that he can't. But he can show her where he found what changed his life from a bleak November to a sunny June.

"Perhaps I could help you a little if you were really determined to find Jesus, but it is you who must find him....If you do search, you will find, with or without any help of mine."

Appendix

Find Reliable Science Information

When you're looking for reliable research about science, there's a money trail that's easy to follow.

People pay taxes to the government. The National Institutes of Health (NIH) provides money to universities, research institutions, and medical centers. This pays for life-saving medical research.

When research is complete, scientists and other researchers write articles about their discoveries. Their articles are submitted to medical journals. The articles are reviewed by peers who analyze and scrutinize the research. If an article is approved for publication, a news release may be written, and then it's approved by the researchers.

The news release is published on the website of the university, medical center, or research institute. Also, it sent to the NIH for their website section called REPORTER.

In addition, the press release is sent to news organizations and journalists. They review the information and decide whether or not to write an article or produce a news segment about the research. That may depend on the timeliness of the research, current trends, or other factors.

Health associations and foundations use the news releases to inform patients, caregivers, and others.

Companies and corporations use the news releases to inform investors and stimulate interest in new products.

Educators, authors, and public speakers refer to the research in their lessons, presentations, and books. Other people post information about the research on their websites and in blogs.

As the information filters down the line, or is recycled, it may contain small or large errors – like those errors that occur when people play the game "telephone." People whisper a message in another person's ear, only to learn that the original message was altered.

When you have questions about research – or supposed research – check the researcher's affiliated institution. Look for a news release or an article. Read the original journal article about their research. If you still can find it, ask more questions.

Here are some shortcuts for online science research:

- Use keywords and include "news release."

- Use keywords and the names of organizations that distribute news releases, such as Newswise, EurekAlert, and Science Daily.

- Use keywords and include "scholarly articles."

- Use keywords and include the word "abstract." An abstract is a required and brief summary of a research article in a journal.

Happy hunting!

Reading Tips: Science or Scripture

This is the **PAGES** reading method. By *doing* something with new information, we can understand more, learn faster, and remember longer.

<u>Preview</u>: Simply read the title, headings, subheadings, or bold words. Read photo captions.

<u>Ask Questions</u>: What is this about? What could be important to me? What's the main point? What do I already know?

<u>Get key words</u>: As you read, circle words that seem important in a sentence or paragraph. When using a computer, copy and paste the text into a Word document. Highlight key words with bold font. Find the meaning of new words and write them down. If the information is difficult, point to the words. Pause and picture what the words mean. When you understand the sentence or section, continue reading normally.

<u>Explain with emotion</u>: At the end of a paragraph, section, or tricky sentence, say what you've just read. Use your own words. Associate or connect the new information to what you already know.

<u>Sort and select</u>: Pick important points to remember. Write them down. Outline them, or draw pictures.

I've adapted this method from Eric Jensen's book *Student Success Secrets*. It engages several brain areas, and it helps me to understand complex information so I can learn quickly and write about science.

Try this little tip. Instead of reading for long periods of time, take one-minute breaks a few times during one hour. It really helps to improve concentration.

Sometimes reading or studying can be tiring. That's because it may require lots of self-control to stay focused and concentrate. The energy to maintain self-control comes from glucose, but it can be depleted quickly by studying or other activities. To get more glucose in your bloodstream, try these tips:

- Exhale and inhale slowly and deeply 10 times
- Exercise or stretch
- Eat fruit or drink water
- Express a strong, positive emotion

Now, here's a shortcut to help you *remember* what you've read.

- Separate big sections of information into small chunks.
- Try to recall recently learned information within 24 hours.
- Recall it again in a few days and then in a week and after a few weeks.

Critical Thinking Questions

Critical thinking skills can help to prevent problems and save time and money. Ask the basic 5-W questions: who, what, where, when, why – and how. Use these reporter's guidelines from William Blundell*'s The Art and Craft of Feature Writing*, based on the *Wall Street Journal Guide*.

1. **BACKGROUND:** Who's the source of this information? Is this source reliable? Is the information second-hand?

2. **SIZE-SCOPE:** What's the importance, meaning, or perspective of this event or news? How many people are affected? What areas are affected?

3. **REASONS:** Why is this news happening now? Is it money, politics, law, health, religion, emotions, or relationships? What are the values or beliefs? How are they typical or different?

4. **IMPACT:** Who is being hurt? Who is being helped? How does this affect finances, politics, emotions, health, religion, or other factors?

5. **COUNTERACTION:** Who or what is working for this or against this new development?

6. **FUTURE:** What do experts say? What do non-experts say? What are the hopes, plans, or goals?

Find and Fix Thinking Traps

It's common for people to use logical fallacies, but doing so can create big problems in certain situations. Here are eleven ways that people may try to influence opinion, use pressure, exert authority, or build power.

1. **EMOTIONAL APPEALS**: Using guilt, fear, anger, or pity to motivate people to think or do something. Remedy: Evaluate strong emotions.

2. **DISTRACTION**: Talking about something unrelated to switch attention from a problem. Remedy: Stay focused.

3. **FALSE AUTHORITY**: Using *misleading* statistics or statements from *qualified* or unqualified authorities. Remedy: Analyze the evidence.

4. **ABSOLUTE WORDS**: Creating false statements by using words such as *always, never, every, only, all, none,* or *must*. Remedy: Listen and read carefully.

5. **FALSE CAUSES AND EFFECTS**: Excusing an action and making it sound reasonable. Remedy: Question excuses.

6. **MISLEADING COMPARISONS**: Comparing two situations that are not related. Remedy: Question comparisons.

7. **LOADED QUESTIONS AND STATEMENTS**: Hiding an opinion in questions, statements, or sarcasm. Remedy: Listen unemotionally and read carefully.

8. **BLACK-AND-WHITE THINKING**: Stating that there are only two alternatives. Remedy: Question alternatives.

9. **ARGUING IN CIRCLES**: Giving an opinion and slightly disguising that opinion in the same argument. Remedy: Ask for specific reasons.

10. **OVER-GENERALIZATION**: Making a conclusion from only a few facts. Remedy: Be specific. Check assumptions.

11. **BANDWAGON**: Using popularity, peer pressure, and social media to make important decisions. Remedy: Think for yourself.

Here is a brief list of remedies for logical fallacies:

- Evaluate strong emotions.

- Stay focused.

- Analyze the evidence.

- Listen unemotionally.

- Read carefully.

- Question excuses.

- Question comparisons.

- Question alternatives.

- Be specific. Check assumptions.

- Think for yourself.

These questions provide an opportunity to practice and remember what you've read about thinking traps.

What were your experiences with logical fallacies?

What ideas from this book might help you in the future?

Who can you share this information with?

Groupthink Symptoms and Remedies

When certain behaviors occur in group settings or high pressure situations, the result may be dysfunctional or irrational thinking. A similar process can occur in close relationships.

SYMPTOMS:

- Overestimating power, expertise, credentials, or immunity
- Fearing criticism, pressure, or punishment
- Withholding important knowledge or opinions
- Labeling questions or opposing opinions as weak or bad
- Requiring uniform thinking
- Mistaking silence as agreement or unity
- Increasing extremism

REMEDIES:

- Support people who listen, inquire, and evaluate
- Encourage critical thinking
- Request diverse opinions
- Challenge logical fallacies or thinking traps
- Reward group success
- Get outside opinions or support if necessary
- Keep your values and stay safe

Although some of the information in this original article has been discussed in this book, other helpful material is included here. In the condensed online article, it has been omitted.

Los Angeles Times

Fear, stress among the poor hinder learning

Students who grow up poor face many obstacles, including overcrowded schools and violent neighborhoods. Fear and stress also may be constants in their lives.

These emotions are a constant for the poverty-stricken. New ideas are emerging to combat the long-term effects.

By Rosemary Clandos, Special to The Times
September 1, 2008

RAISED IN poverty, Dr. Shauna Blake Collins fought fear during nearly 14 years of education. A dropout from a South-Central Los Angeles high school, she earned a GED diploma at 22, became a licensed vocational nurse, a registered nurse, and finally, at 41, a physician. Confidence came only during the last two years of medical school.

"Every step of the way, I was petrified," says the Winnetka mother of two toddlers, who recently graduated from UCLA's David Geffen School of Medicine. "The pressure I put on myself made me paralyzed."

Students who grow up amid economic insecurity often face many obstacles: overcrowded schools, lack of enrichment activities, violent neighborhoods. Fear and stress can be two more problems. Brain science is showing how these emotions have effects on the brain and how they can directly impede learning. Some scientists and educators are suggesting ways in which kids and college students can combat the long-lasting effects of poverty-related stress.

Taking over thoughts

In response to fear or stress, the brain quickly releases adrenaline and cortisol, activating the heart, blood vessels and brain for life-saving action -- fighting or running. The brain gives the threat priority over anything else -- including schoolwork -- and it creates powerful memories to help prevent future threats. "All families experience stress, but poor families experience a lot of it," says Martha Farah, psychology professor at the University of Pennsylvania.

For 20 years, David Diamond, a neuroscience professor at the University of South Florida, has studied the effects of stress-related hormones in rats. He found that high cortisol levels affect the hippocampus -- a key learning center in the brain -- in three ways. They suppress electrical activity, decrease efficiency and reduce new cell growth.

These effects, thought likely to occur in humans as well, might be one reason it's hard for impoverished students to concentrate and learn -- especially if there is extra stress, violence or abuse in the child's environment, Diamond says.

In a 2006 issue of Brain Research, Farah reported that growing up in poverty affects thinking processes associated with several brain systems. Sixty healthy middle-school students matched for age, gender and ethnicity but of different socioeconomic status took tests that challenged brain areas responsible for specific cognitive abilities. Researchers found that children from low-income homes had significantly lower scores in areas of language, long-term and short-term memory, and attention.

Research, Farah says, suggests that the effect of stress on the brain may be the reason for these detected differences and disadvantages.

Fear also interferes with learning. A study published in the February online journal of Social Cognitive and Affective Neuroscience shows that students raised in low-income homes have stronger fear reactions -- with potential consequences for concentration.

In the study, 33 healthy undergraduate students viewed pictures of facial expressions -- angry, surprised and neutral -- while MRI imaging measured their brain activity. For students raised in low-income homes, the pictures of angry faces triggered a greater response in the amygdala, a brain region that processes fear and anger.

"Growing up in a socially disadvantaged environment often exposes people to threats to their health and well-being," says Peter Gianaros, an assistant professor of psychiatry and psychology at the University of Pittsburgh, who headed the research.

Changing the brain

There are science-supported ways to mitigate these accentuated fear and stress responses and nurture the brain, researchers and educators say.

"Change the experience, and you change the brain," says San Diego-based educator Eric Jensen, author of a 2006 book "Enriching the Brain: How to Maximize Every Learner's

Potential," who has developed a teachers' training program, "Enriching the Brains of Poverty." "Many good schools have shown they can create experiences that change the brain for the better."

Among those experiences:

* Targeted preparation. To help children succeed in school, Jensen teaches educators to build students' brain capacity in areas shown by science to be lagging: attention, long-term effort, memory, processing skills and sequencing skills. He recommends a slate of activities for each -- for example, compelling stories, theater arts and fine-motor tasks all build attention skills, he says.

* Foster a mind-set of hope, determination and optimism -- and security. There are many ways to foster hope, Jensen says, including asking about and affirming a student's dreams, bringing successful students back to talk to new ones, giving useful feedback on schoolwork and teaching students how to set and monitor their own goals.

Studies by Dr. Helen Mayberg of Emory University have reported lower activity in the thinking parts of the brain in people with depression, and research has uncovered brain changes as people get better, either with medical treatments or psychotherapy.

And in a study to be published this month in Neuron, Dr. Eric Kandel, a Nobel laureate and neuroscience professor at Columbia University, found that positive emotions -- safety and security -- affect learning capabilities of mice.

"Behaviors and thoughts that relate to hope, love and happiness can change the brain -- just as fear, stress and anxiety can change it," Kandel says. "It's completely symmetrical."

* Meditation. This has been proven in studies to lower stress.

* Social connectedness. According to Diamond's work at the Veterans Hospital in Tampa, Fla., "When people are experiencing strong stress, they recover much better when they have social support than when they are socially isolated," he says.

Jensen recommends mentoring programs for children and student groups.

* Take control. "Feeling helpless increases stress hormones," Diamond says. To offset learned helplessness and develop a sense of control, Jensen advised students to learn time-management skills and goal setting -- and reward small accomplishments.

* Exercise. "Exercise stimulates and energizes the brain to more efficiently process information. Exercise actually makes more brain cells," Diamond says. Sports, aerobic exercise, yoga, dance, walking and even exercising the smaller muscles used for playing a musical instrument can change the brain. Music is calming, Diamond says. "If you feel better, you learn better."

* Eat well. Marian Diamond, a neuroscientist and professor at UC Berkeley, has been using dietary changes to improve the learning capabilities of orphans and impoverished children in Cambodia. For students living in poverty in the U.S., she said, "Be sure you're getting good sources of protein and calcium. Each day, eat an egg -- or egg whites – a glass of milk, and take a multivitamin." Other researchers recommend cutting back on sugar and smoking because they raise cortisol levels.

* Spirituality. In the January 2003 journal Urban Education, researchers reported that African American and Latino high school

seniors who reported that they were very religious and were raised in intact families scored as well as white students on most achievement tests. "The achievement gap disappeared," says William Jeynes, an education professor at Cal State Long Beach.

Neuroplasticity can occur with music. In this article, the author of "This is Your Brain on Music," David Levitin, explains more.

Feeling blue? Try a dose of gospel music

By Rosemary Clandos

Appeared in print: Friday, Dec. 4, 2009

The next time the choir director says get up and dance, do it. It's a chance to build your neuropathways for hope. Audiences will get an opportunity on Sunday when Andiel Brown leads the University of Oregon Gospel Choir and Ensembles at Beall Hall at 5 p.m.

Black gospel music has a history of building hope. For generations, the music has been a backbone for strength and courage. And in today's tough economic times, there's a lot of benefit in the music. It's not just the lyrics and message that make it work — it's also the repetition and the movement. Plus, there's science related to it.

People who sing together experience the release of oxytocin, a hormone engendering a feeling of trust. Also, prolactin and dopamine, other soothing and feel-good hormones, may be released, and the effects of those chemicals can linger, said Daniel Levitin, a professor of neuroscience and psychology at McGill

University in Montreal and author of "This is Your Brain on Music."

"Gospel music reinforces the neuropathways associated with positive thinking and positive outcomes," said Levitin, who earned his doctoral degree from the UO in 1996. He also wrote the New York Times best-seller "The World in Six Songs."

"Gospel music distracts people when they're feeling blue and rewires the brain to accommodate positive biochemicals," he said. "That changes the structure and function of the brain."

It's something people have been doing for a long time.

Religious music, in general, has been a way for African-Americans to deal with their problems when they don't have a lot of other recourses in society, said Jacqueline Cogdell DjeDje, professor of ethnomusicology at UCLA and author of "California Soul: Music of African-Americans in the West."

She said that historically, gospel music has always represented the good news — you're able to move into new arenas, new status, new beginnings. It reflects the experience of blacks when they were free. It's different from spirituals that were sung during slavery.

"Tragedy after tragedy, people would go to the church and sing," said Andiel Brown, director of gospel choirs and ensembles at the UO who will be conducting at Sunday's concert. " 'We shall overcome' is a gospel song in itself. We will not just overcome, we will prosper and we will succeed. Nowadays, the music brings us back to that."

The UO gospel choir began in the mid-'80s under the directorship of John Gainer. Other directors held the position before Brown accepted the post two years ago.

"Gospel music is part of the American culture, and people in the Northwest know very little about it," said Brown, a former UO football running back who recently won a local "Billie Jean" dance contest. "I'm definitely trying to get the spirit of the culture and inspiration out there. The music stimulates unity in the community."

The performance this Sunday should also stimulate a lot of high energy.

"I've included a lot of upbeat songs — no one wants to come in from the cold and hear slow songs," he said. The choir will perform several numbers by Kirk Franklin, Fred Hammond and the Clarke Sisters.

To get the most out of gospel music, Brown said: "Let yourself loose in the music. Let go of problems and inhibitions. If people choose not to worry about how they look or how others may perceive them, that's when they get the most benefit out of the experience."

Wendy Plueard, a full-time caregiver for an elderly relative with a developmental disability, recently heard Brown and the choir perform at the Springfield library.

"I love the music, it feeds my soul and encourages me," she said.

An exhilarating emotion or experience can alter the neuro-configuration of the brain, where a bunch of boring experiences

160

might not. So it's not sufficient to simply sing, you have to be engaged and have it be meaningful to you, Levitin said.

Repetition also helps to build neuropathways for hope. Levitin explained that it's the key for the brain to alter itself. "If you want to change the brain reliably, you don't do something once, you engage it on a regular basis. So then the neurons associated with this activity start to fire preferentially and at a lower threshold."

Now here's the fun part — dancing.

Movement reinforces the neuropathways. "When you're moving you have more neurons firing and involved, and that makes the activity more memorable and engaging. So the emotion will be better recalled," Levitin said.

"The same part of the brain that's related to emotion is also related to body movement. Emotions can trigger motion or movement. It's no accident that motion is part of the word emotion," Levitin said. "And it's no accident that muse — meaning inspiration and hope — is part of the word music."

Yet, there's another trick to this hope business, and it was summed up on a banner written in a church in an impoverished African-American community in Detroit. It read, "Praise God Anyhow." In other words: Do a positive behavior in the midst of a negative emotion.

"Gospel music is a reminder that there is hope, and that fills me with joy," said Brown. "You see me going around singing and dancing all the time. It's a great tool, a great way to keep people's spirits uplifted."

So, in this season when employment is down — but hope is hiring — here's a chance to get a good job.

Questions for Study Groups

1. How did the information in this book relate to what you already knew about brain science?

2. What misconceptions did you have about brain science?

3. What did you gain from reading this book?

4. What information have you *already* used from this book?

5. What additional information would you like to use?

6. Who else could be helped by the ideas in this book?

7. How could you pray for people who upset you?

8. What causes you to think of a loving God?

Questions for Study Groups

Create your own questions.

Write Your Own Life Stories

After reading stories in this book, some people may want to write about their life stories. Here are a few suggestions to get you started sharing your experiences, strength, and hope.

1. Think of a story you want to tell. List important points in that story. Organize those points. Arrange them in order of time, location, importance, or any other category.

2. Draft the story. Write quickly. Include emotions, dialogue, and sensory details. **Don't edit at this point.** Frequently save your work on the computer. Take a break.

3. Revise your work. Start by checking the organization of your paragraphs. List the key words in each paragraph to make sure that the ideas flow logically. Delete unnecessary information. Check the paragraphs, sentences, words, and punctuation.

For detailed information, check online for books and videos.

Recommended Books and Videos

Books

The Brain That Changes Itself, by Norman Doidge

How God Changes Your Brain, by Andrew Newberg and Mark Robert Waldman

Groupthink, by Cass R. Sunstein and Reid Hastie

The Woman Who Changed Her Brain: How I Left My Learning Disability Behind, by Barbara Arrowsmith-Young

Change Your Brain, Change Your Life, by Daniel G. Amen

In Search of Memory: The Emergence of a New Science of Mind, by Eric R. Kandel

Videos

Videos that include the above authors are available on YouTube. For basic or advanced information about neuroscience, check out videos on Khan Academy. Look for other videos on YouTube. The ones created for kids can be a great starting place for learning more about neuroscience.

Acknowledgements

Thank you to Jesus for hope and help. I could not have written this book without you, and I could not have met the challenges that I faced without you.

Thanks goes to Pam Fazalare, Val Rope, Sarah Doe, Debbie Amaral, and Christye Johnson for laughter, encouragement, and long-term prayers.

Eileen Richmond, thank you for your prayers, support, and diligent editing. Your efforts made a tremendous impact on this book. You are a godsend. Nancy Peltcs, I appreciate your keen eye for line editing. For the last-minute reviews, thank you Sue Hudson, Terry Hassman-Paulin, and June Abramian. Photo artist Kristen Kay, thanks for the cover image.

Thank you dearest daughters, Elizabeth and Christina, for encouraging me to stop using bullet points to describe my past and to start disclosing. Elizabeth, your broad perspective, witty feedback, and encouragement were heartening. Christina, thanks for your sweet persistence, design tips, and content editing.

To my sisters, thank you. Barbara Morrish, I appreciate your encouragement and editing skills. During my early stages of faith, your loving patience in the midst of my anger was vital.

Kris Khurana, I appreciate your support and insight. Dolores Wylie, thanks for your love and timely input.

A big thank-you goes to Christopher Guiley, Gary Morrish, Maria Fischer, and everyone else who cheered for me. You're a blessing!

With heartfelt gratitude, I thank Ellen Freeman. When my mom was on hospice, I received a picture of you reading part of this book to her. I learned you did this often. The image gave me hope that people could benefit from the book if only I would finish it.

About the Author

Rosemary (Rosie) Clandos has written about cancer research, nanobiotechnology, microelectromechanical systems, and numerous other science-related topics. Her weekly column on health and nutrition appeared in more than 35 newspapers. In addition, she reported on subjects ranging from music to business. Rosie is passionate about teaching study strategies and critical thinking skills. Learn more at RosemaryClandos.com

Action Steps

If you need professional help, please find it.

- Association for Anxiety and Depression www.adaa.org

- Association for Behavioral and Cognitive Therapies www.abct.org

- National Suicide Prevention Lifeline 1-800-273-TALK (8255)

If you're looking for a church, check their websites for more information or recorded sermons.

Prayer lines are available at many churches and ministries. Search on the Internet for "telephone prayer lines". Some lines are open 24/7.

It takes time to retrain the brain. If you like the concepts in this book, practice them. (I will, too.) Write about your own experiences. Re-read the book every once in awhile.

If you want to share how this book helped you, or if you'd like to schedule a speaking engagement, please contact: RosemaryClandos@gmail.com.

"Tell me, what is it you plan to do with

your one wild and precious life?"

Mary Oliver